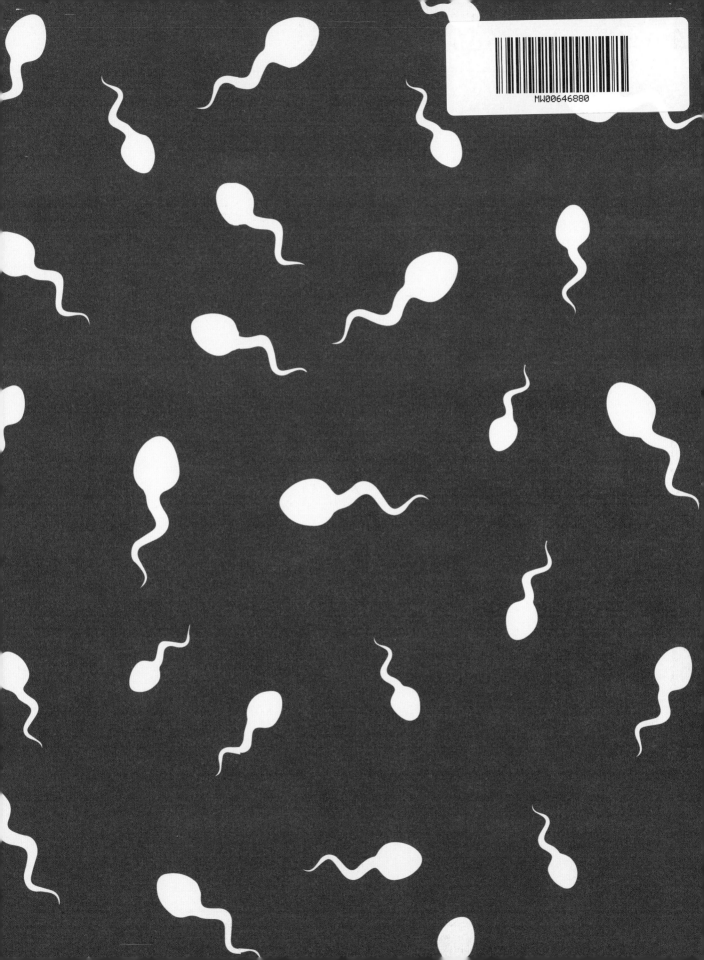

To the trillions of lives lost through
cortical reaction (Google it)

MASCOT® BOOKS

www.mascotbooks.com

The Sperm That Came in Second

For more information, please contact:
Mascot Books
620 Herndon Parkway #320
Herndon, VA 20170
info@mascotbooks.com

CPSIA Code: PRT0121A
ISBN-13: 978-1-68401-674-7

Printed in the United States

The Sperm That Came in Second

Written by Jay Provo

Illustrated by Kyle Donovan

Once upon a time,
a couple was wooing.
All over the house,
their bodies were stewing!

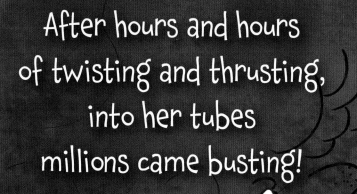

After hours and hours
of twisting and thrusting,
into her tubes
millions came busting!

They raced against time,
they raced for the ages,
through darkness and slime,
and many terrible stages...

Along their journey
some would go insane.
Some didn't make it—left as a stain,
but most of the swimmers would die in pain.

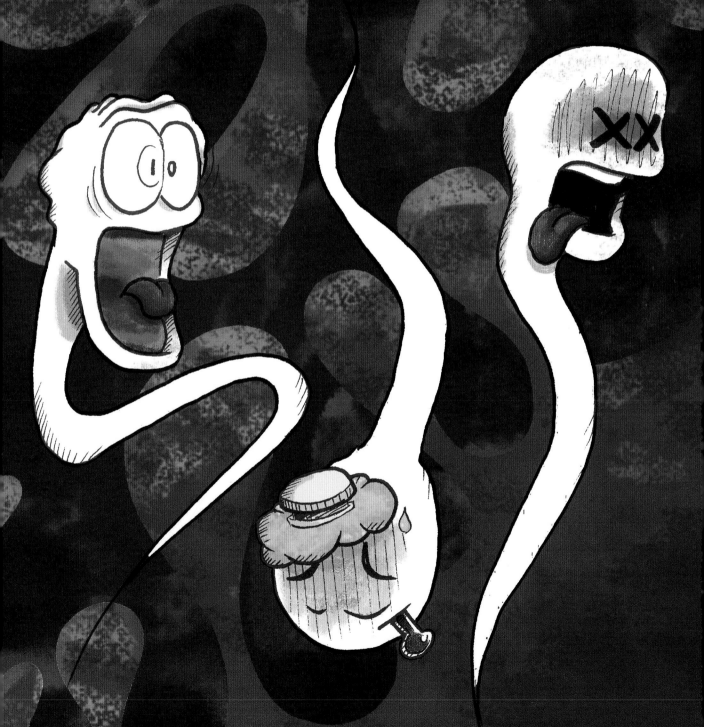

Those remaining pushed on,
conquering impossible mazes,
running the race against incredible odds
and through remarkably tight spaces.

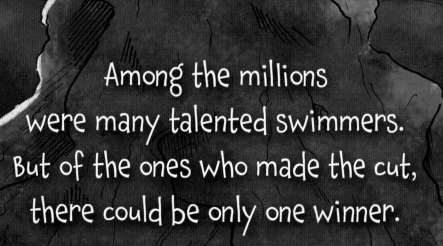

Among the millions
were many talented swimmers.
But of the ones who made the cut,
there could be only one winner.

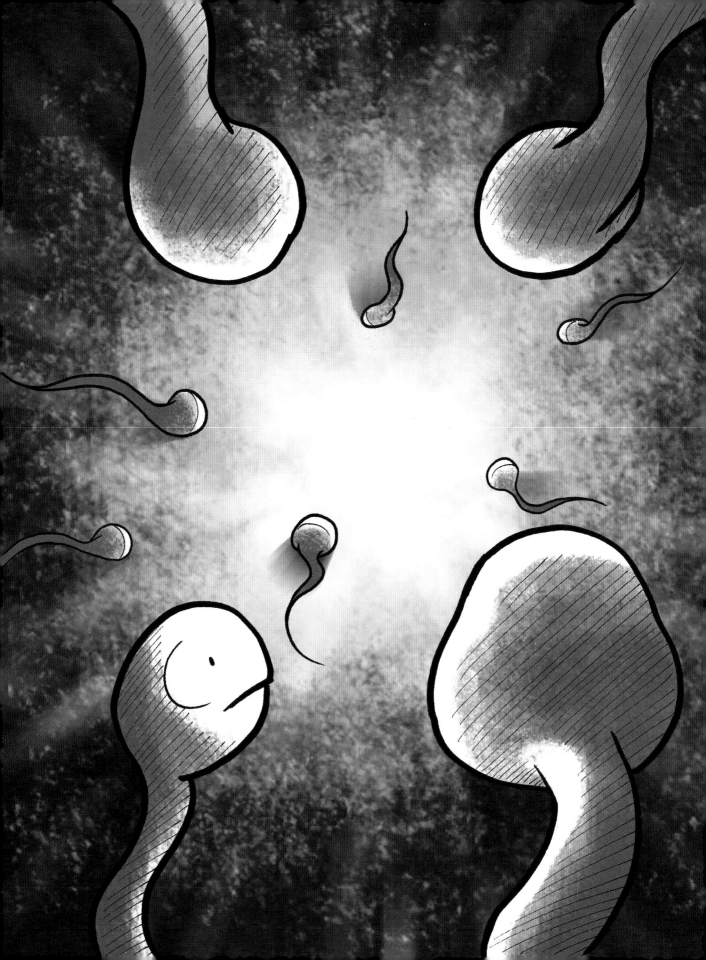

For many, hope was lost
until a bright light appeared in the distance
telling them to go on at all costs,
giving them hope in an instant.

Suddenly, a burst of energy
sparked in just a few.
It was Jane, Frank, and little Bob
who came barreling through!

They pushed and they pulled,
they wiggled with all their might,
and they fought and they thrashed,
for there could be only one winner on this lucky
night.

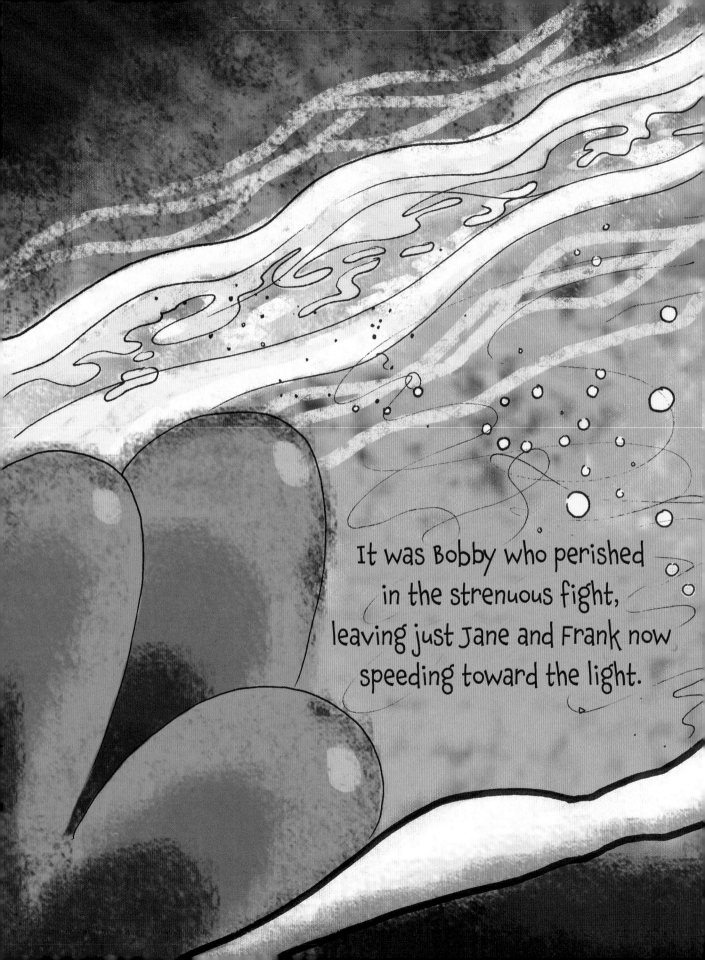

It was Bobby who perished
in the strenuous fight,
leaving just Jane and Frank now
speeding toward the light.

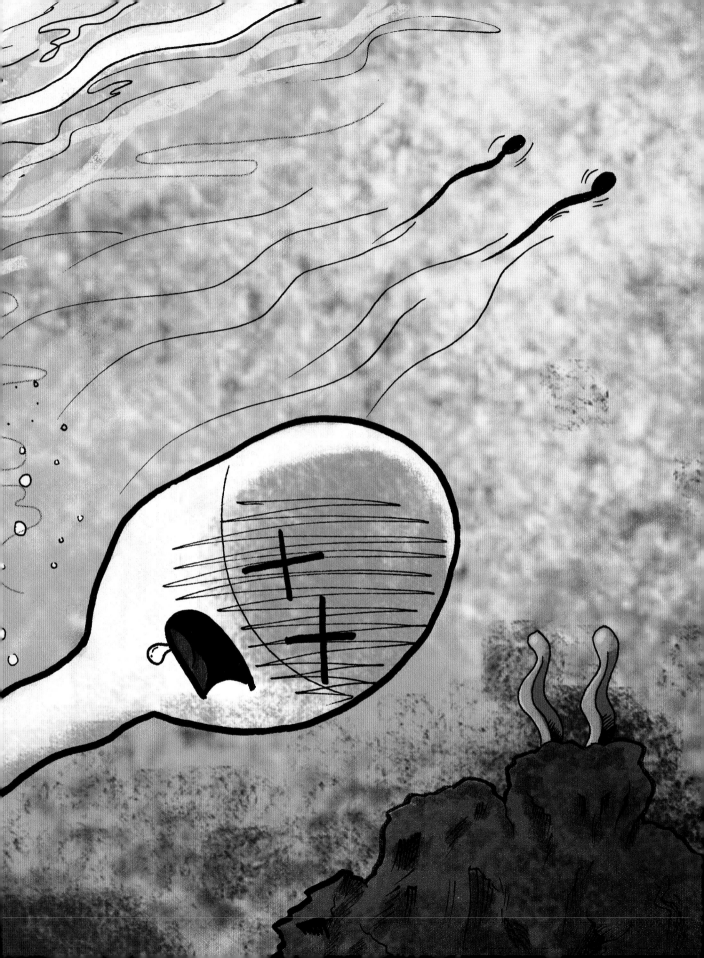

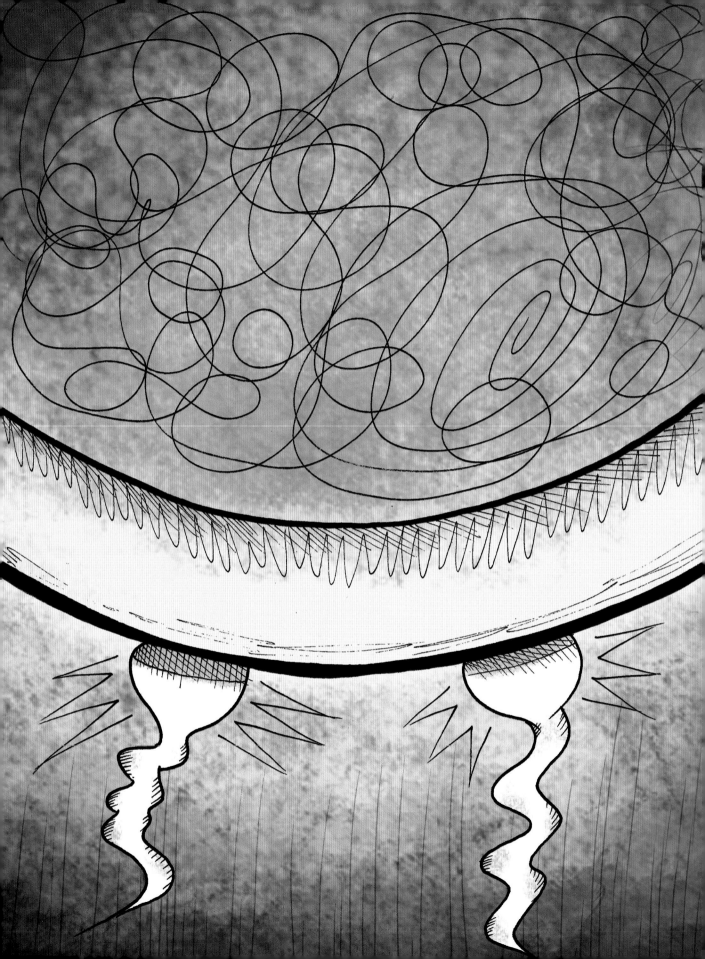

Swimming too fast,
they hit a wall and felt a terrible pain,
but they kept pushing and pushing
with the force of a train.

At the end of the battle
it was Frank who had won.
Leaving Jane behind,
he knew she was done.

But Jane would not accept defeat,
she would not surrender.

"I don't belong in a sock or towel.
I'll determine the gender!"

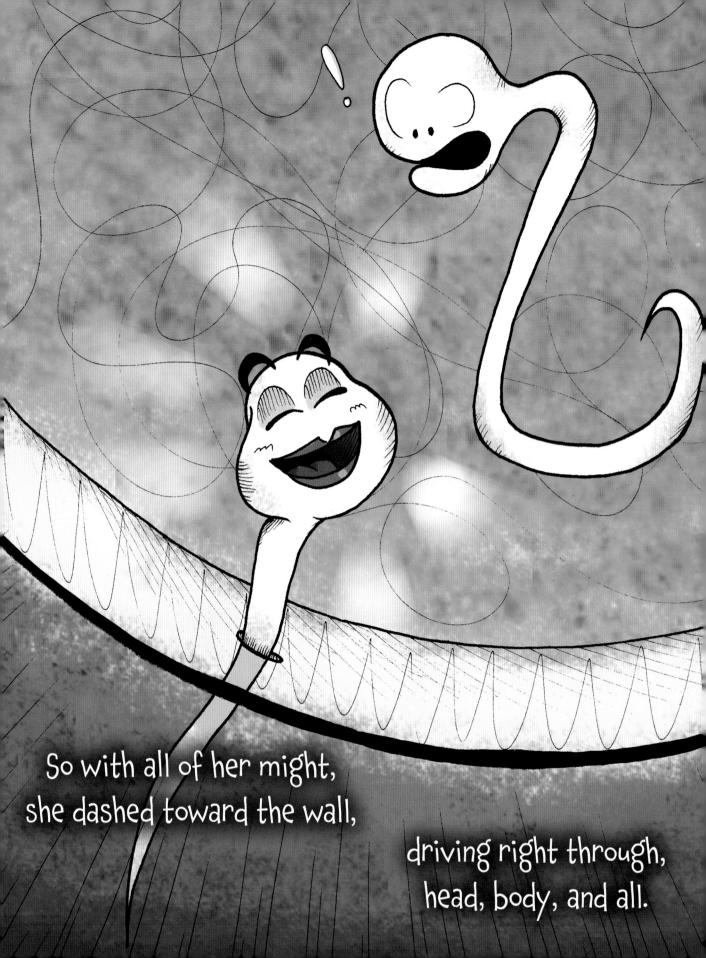

So with all of her might,
she dashed toward the wall,

driving right through,
head, body, and all.

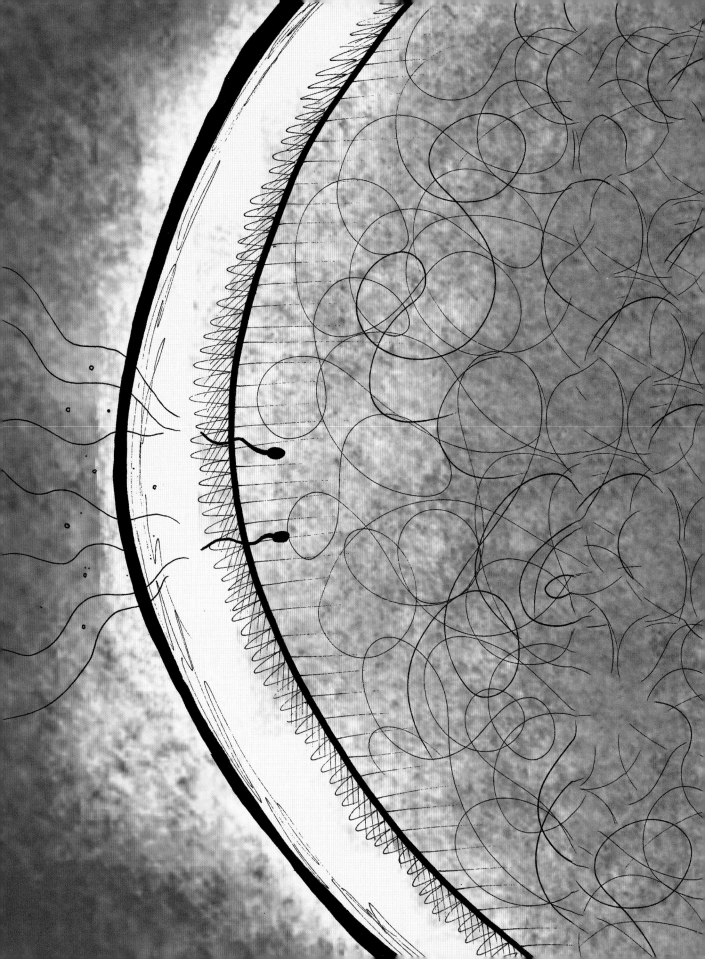

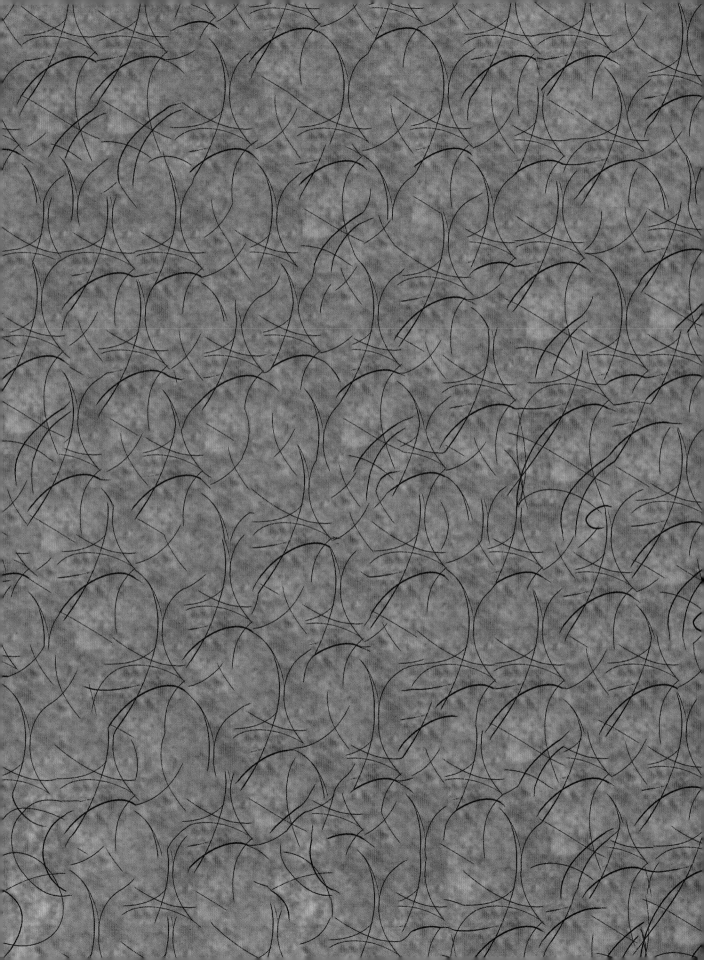

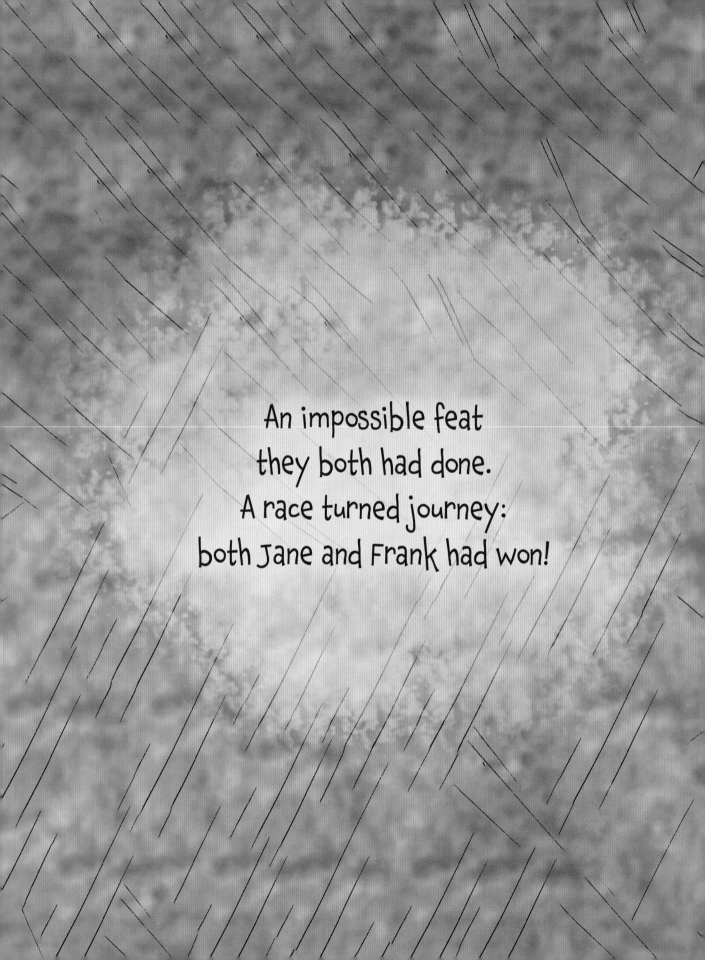

An impossible feat
they both had done.
A race turned journey:
both Jane and Frank had won!

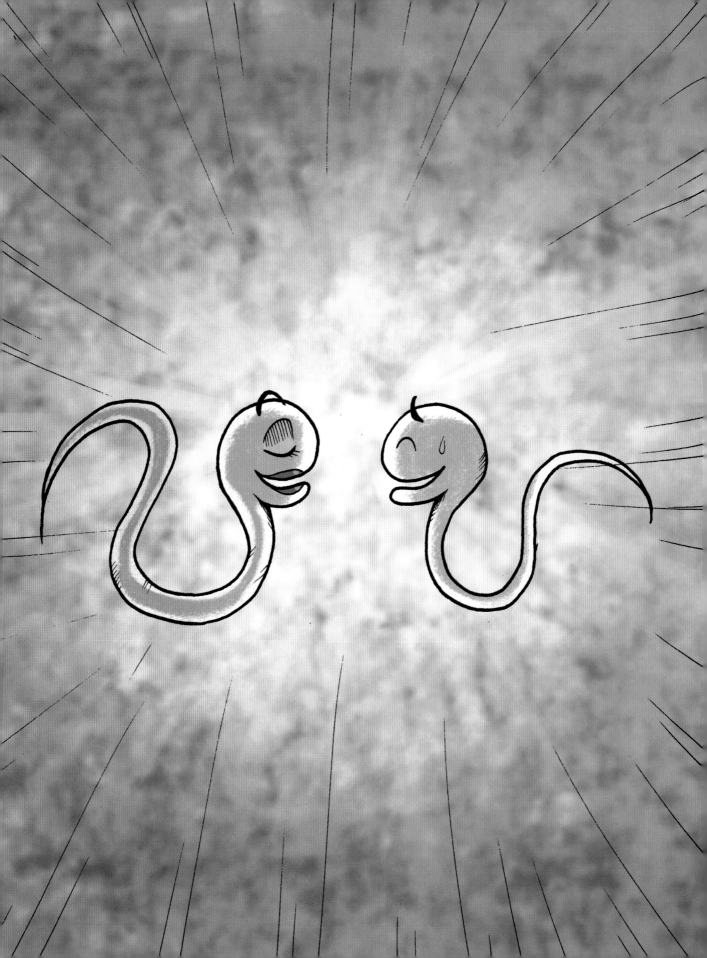

The next month at the doctor,
they felt some cool pressure.
The parents could see them!
"Looks like twins in your future!"

As the picture grew clearer,
the doc said, "This is it!"
When they saw Frank and Jane, one whispered,

"Oh Shit".

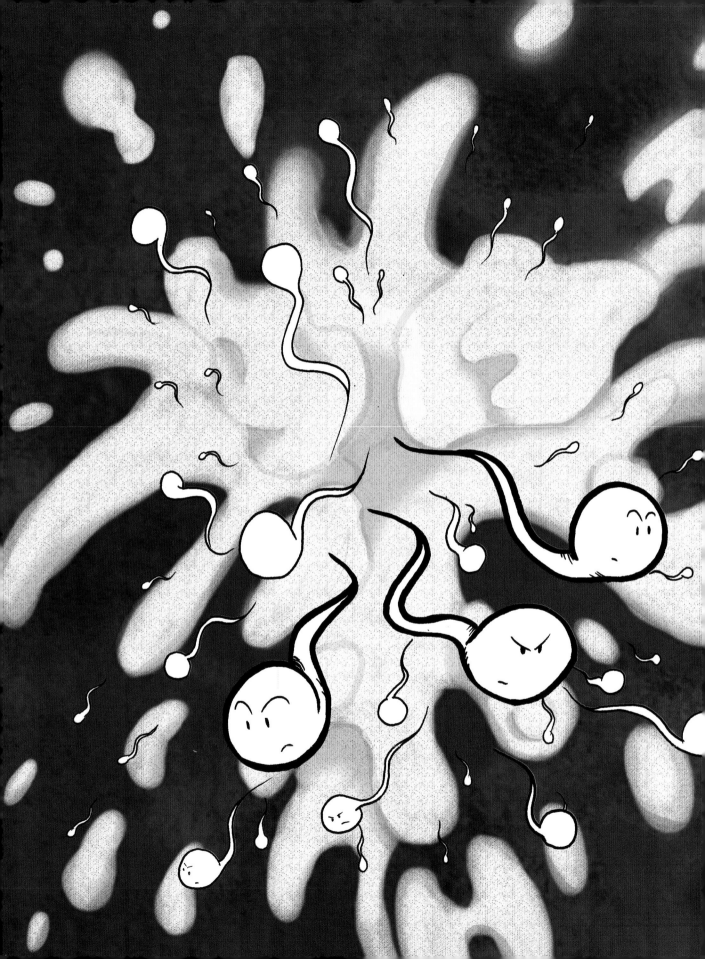

About the Author

Jay Provo is a new author who lives with some pets in the United States. His dreams of mediocrity as a child have come to remarkable fruition. Besides having an excessive uneasiness and impending sense of doom, he casually goes about his meaningless existence like most mindless automatons. He has heated leather theater seats that are disassembled and stored in his brother's basement because he needed a pullout couch to make it look like he occasionally welcomes company. If he's ever lost, don't tell him where to go because he might end up somewhere he wants to be.

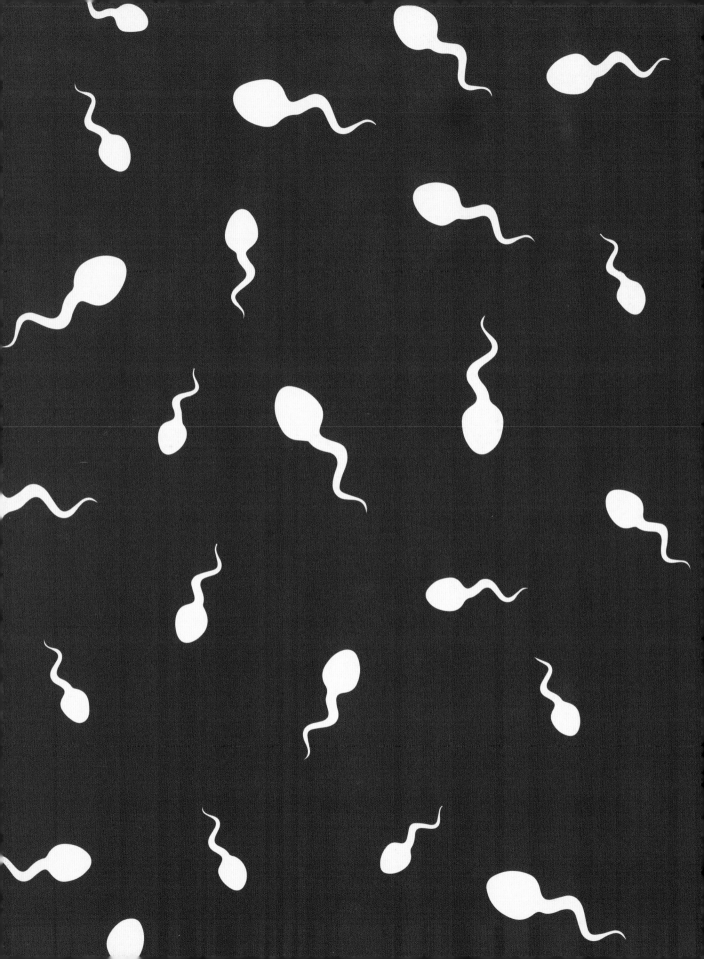

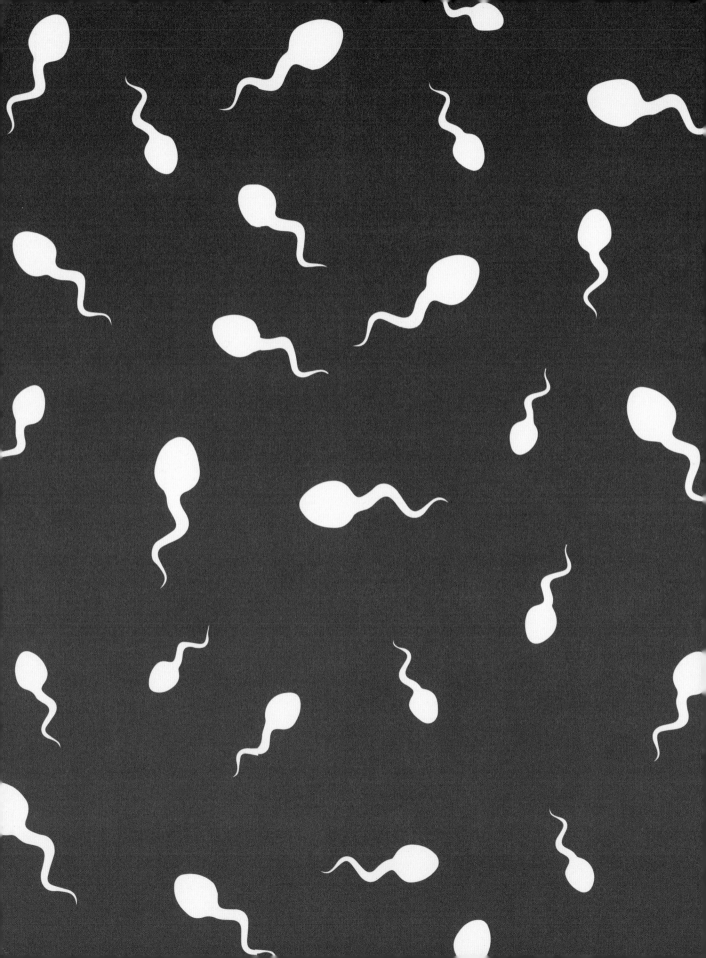